Bon Appetit

We hope that you can take the spirit

of the Olympic Games home with you and,

through cooking and sharing international

recipes, spread the warmth of friendship

and fine dining that we wish you in our

Centennial Celebration Cookbook.

ATHENS, GREECE
1896

PARIS, FRANCE
1900

ST. LOUIS, USA
1904

LONDON, ENGLAND
1908

STOCKHOLM, SWEDEN
1912

ANTWERP, BELGIUM
1920

PARIS, FRANCE
1924

AMSTERDAM, HOLLAND
1928

LOS ANGELES, USA
1932

BERLIN, GERMANY
1936

LONDON, ENGLAND
1948

HELSINKI, FINLAND
1952

MELBOURNE, AUSTRALIA
1956

ROME, ITALY
1960

TOKYO, JAPAN
1964

MEXICO CITY, MEXICO
1968

MUNICH, GERMANY
1972

MONTRÉAL, CANADA
1976

MOSCOW, USSR
1980

LOS ANGELES, USA
1984

SEOUL, KOREA
1988

BARCELONA, SPAIN
1992

ATLANTA, USA
1996

Atlanta 1996

TM © 1992 ACOG

1

Athens, Greece

Finikia
Cookies

1/2 cup butter or margarine
1/2 cup crisco (solid crisco)
1/2 cup vegetable oil
1/2 cup sugar
2 egg yolks
1 tsp vanilla
1/2 cup orange juice
1 tsp baking powder
1/2 tsp baking soda
1/4 tsp salt
1/4 tsp cinnamon
1/4 tsp cloves
Flour
1/2 cup chopped nuts
1 cup honey and 1 tbsp water
Ground walnuts
Cinnamon

Beat butter, crisco and oil until fluffy. Add sugar, egg yolks, vanilla, orange juice. Mix in baking powder, baking soda, spices and enough flour to make soft dough. Add nuts. Bake 12-15 minutes at 375° F. Do not brown top.

Heat honey and water to boiling point. Dip cookies in honey. Put in strainer. Roll them in ground walnuts and cinnamon sugar. (Could use cookie press.)

Baklava
Filled Pastry

2 lbs phyllo pastry
2 cups sweet butter, melted
1-1/2 lbs walnuts or pistachios, finely
   chopped
4 cups sugar
1 tsp fresh lemon juice
Orange-flower water or rosewater
   (optional)

Butter a baking tray of adequate size for the sheets of dough and with sides at least 2" high. Pile up 4 sheets of dough and brush liberally with butter. Repeat, buttering every fourth sheet, until the pile is 1" high. Spread evenly with nuts. Again pile up sheets of dough for another inch, buttering every fourth one and using up all of the butter. Cut diagonally to make diamond shapes about 1" wide. Bake in preheated very slow oven (250° F.) for 2-1/2 hours. While hot from oven, pour on syrup made of 2 cups water and 4 cups sugar cooked until thick, then sprinkled with lemon juice. An additional sprinkling of orange-flower water is optional. Cool before serving. Makes 20 or more servings.

The Acropolis and Parthenon
Photo by Lee Snider/Photo Images

Crepes

3/4 cup white flour

1 tsp baking powder

1/2 tsp salt

2 tbsp powdered sugar

2/3 cup milk

1/3 cup water

1/2 tsp vanilla

2 tbsp oil

2 eggs

Combine flour, sugar, baking powder and salt together in bowl. Beat eggs, milk, water and vanilla together. Add to remaining ingredients. Beat mixture lightly. Heat oil until almost smoky in skillet. Pour small quantity of batter in and rotate pan so batter spreads evenly. Cook until light brown; turn and brown other side. You can spread almost anything on crepes and roll up (jam or preserves; cream cheese and chopped nuts; canned sweetened cherries, blueberries and sour cream are a few suggestions). If you desire, add powdered sugar. Serves 4.

Soupe à l'oignon
French Onion Soup

4 large onions, sliced thin

2 tbsp butter

2 cans condensed beef broth

1 soup can water

1 tsp Worcestershire sauce

8 to 12 slices from tiny french loaf (or hard rolls), toasted

4 to 6 1/4" thick slices swiss or parmesan cheese

Cook onions in butter until tender but not brown. Add broth, water, and Worcestershire. Cover; simmer 20 minutes. Season with salt and pepper. Pour soup into ovenproof bowls to nearly full. Float two slices toasted bread atop each. Cover each bowl with a thick slice of cheese. Place on foil (to catch cheese drips); broil 4 inches from heat just until cheese starts to melt and turn golden on edges, about 4 minutes. Serves 4 to 6.

The Eifel Tower
Photo by J. Joseph

St. Louis, United States

1904

Carol's BBQ Baby Back Ribs

Rib Braising Broth:

- 4 quarts beef broth
- 1 tbsp paprika
- 1-1/2 tbsp cayenne pepper
- 1-1/2 tbsp ground cumin
- 3 tbsp tabasco
- 1 tsp garlic
- 3 slabs baby back ribs

BBQ Sauce:

- 156 oz. Heinz ketchup
- 8 oz. rendered beef fat

Heat to a simmer and add:

- 7 oz. liquid smoke
- 10 oz. Lea & Perrin worcestershire
- 5 cloves garlic crushed or chopped very fine
- 2 cups light brown sugar
- 1 tsp salt
- 2 tbsp black pepper
- 2 tbsp cayenne pepper
- 4 tbsp vinegar

Simmer until thick and flavors blend. In large stock pot simmer all ingredients except ribs for 1/2 hour. Add whole slabs of baby back ribs to stock. Simmer for 45 min. to 1 hour. Turn off heat and let soak for 1/2 hour or until ready to use. Place slabs over low heat coals bone side down first. Coat the meat side with BBQ sauce and cover with lid. Turn and coat again after 15 min. Total cooking time about 45 min. May need to turn often if coals are too hot.

Potato Casserole

- 5 lbs potatoes peeled and sliced
- 2 large onions sliced
- 1 lb. slab bacon
- 2 large square aluminum pans

Peel and slice potatoes 1/4" thick. Line bottom of 1 pan with bacon, onion slices, potatoes, salt and pepper. Repeat and top with bacon. Place second pan on top and over-wrap with foil to seal. Bake in 350° F oven for 45 min. and flip pan over to brown top of bacon. Bake for 1 hr. Can also cook on grill, turning more often.

Gateway Arch
Photo by J. Joseph

4

Recipes courtesy of Carol Luman

Oxtail with Grapes

This dish should be cooked
the day before

3 lbs jointed oxtail
1 tbsp vegetable oil
1 oz. butter
1 large onion, diced
2 large carrots, finely diced
1 clove of garlic, chopped
1 large wine glass of dry sherry
1 tbsp tomato purée
1 bay leaf
1 tsp chopped thyme
salt
freshly ground black pepper
1 lb. seedless grapes

Trim off excess fat from the oxtail, wash and dry well. Heat together the oil and butter in a heavy based pan and brown the meat with the onion, carrots and garlic. Strain off surplus fat, pour over the sherry and flame. Stir in the tomato purée and add the herbs. Season to taste with salt and pepper and pour in enough cold water to cover. Bring up to boil, cover with a lid and cook very slowly for at least 2 hours. When the oxtail is tender, remove the pan from the heat and allow to cool. Skin off the fat from the surface and discard the bay leaf. To serve, add the grapes and reheat gently until the fruit is soft, about 10-15 minutes. Serves 6.

Caramel Puddings

1/4 cup sugar
3 tbsp cornstarch
1/4 tsp salt
2 cups milk
1-1/2 tsp vanilla

Caramel syrup:
  1/4 cup sugar
  1/2 cup boiling water
Caramel trim:
  1/2 cup sugar

Make caramel syrup: melt sugar in heavy skillet, stirring until rich brown. Remove from heat. Slowly add boiling water. Return to heat; stir until smooth.

Combine sugar, cornstarch, and salt in saucepan; blend in milk. Stir in caramel syrup. Cook and stir over medium heat until thick. Cook 2 minutes more. Add vanilla. Pour into bowls.

For caramel trim, melt sugar in heavy skillet over low heat, stirring constantly. When golden, remove from heat and immediately drizzle over puddings. The syrup hardens to crackly "candy."

Big Ben
Courtesy of The British Consulate, Atlanta

Stockholm, Sweden

Svensla Kottbullar
Swedish Meatballs

1 lb. lean ground beef
1 small onion, grated and preferably
   red
1 tsp salt
1-1/4 tsp ground allspice
1 egg yolk
1/2 cup unsweetened bread, soaked in
   1/2 cup hot water
butter for frying

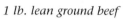

Combine ground beef, onion, salt, allspice, egg yolk and soaked bread. Mix thoroughly until smooth. Shape one small meatball and fry in butter in heavy skillet to check taste. Correct seasoning with salt and allspice as desired. Shape meatballs. This is easier if you dip your hands in cold water or use 2 spoons. Fry meatballs, 8 to 10 at a time, in melted butter over moderate heat. By shaking skillet now and then, the meatballs will retain their round form and will brown evenly on all sides. Serve with mashed potatoes and lingonberry or cranberry preserves. Serves 4 to 6.

Hanna's Appelkaka
Hanna's Apple Cake

A most popular dessert in Sweden

3/4 cup ground blanched almonds
3 to 4 bitter almonds, ground
3-1/2 oz butter
6 tbsp sugar
1/2 lemon, juice and grated rind
2 egg yolks
3 egg whites
6 to 8 apples, precooked with sugar or
   raw and thinly sliced

Preheat oven to 400° F. Place the well-drained apples in a shallow buttered baking dish. Cream butter and sugar until light and fluffy. Gradually blend in egg yolks, ground almonds, lemon rind and juice. Beat egg whites until stiff but not dry. Carefully fold into almond batter. Spread batter over apples. Bake for 15 minutes until golden. Best warm! Serves 5 to 6.

View of the old city
Photo by Lee Snider/Photo Images

Recipes courtesy of The Embassy of Sweden

- VII OLYMPIADE -
ANVERS (BELGIQUE)
1920 AOUT-SEPTEMBRE 1920

Waterzooi de Poulet à la Gantoise
Chicken Stew, Ghent Style

2 celery stalks
2 medium onions
1 carrot
1 leek
3 tbsp. butter
1-1/2 quarts water
2 sprigs parsley
salt, pepper and nutmeg to taste
1 stewing chicken (3 lbs) cut into
   serving pieces
2 tbsp flour
2 egg yolks
1/2 cup light cream
1 tsp chopped parsley

Chop celery stalks, onions, carrot and the white portion of the leek. Simmer for 15 minutes in covered stew pan with 1 tbsp butter. Add water, bring to a boil, then add the parsley sprigs, salt, pepper and grated nutmeg to taste and the chicken. Cook over low heat for about 1 hour. Strain stock, reserve vegetables, keep chicken warm.

Melt 2 tbsp butter, add flour and 2-1/2 cups chicken stock. Stir until thick, but do not boil. Mix egg yolks into cream, add carefully to sauce. Correct seasoning. Add reserved vegetables and chicken, boned and skinned. Serve in deep plates, sprinkled with parsley and accompanied by boiled potatoes. Serves 4.

Gaufres Chantilly
Waffles Chantilly

4 egg yolks
1 cup milk
1 tsp dried or fresh yeast
2/3 cup flour
1 pinch salt
1 tbsp sugar
7 tbsp butter

Beat the cold milk with the egg yolks. Dissolve the yeast in 2 tbsp warm water. Sift the flour into a bowl with the salt and sugar and gradually beat in the egg yolks and milk with the yeast and the softened butter. Leave the batter to rise until it is double in bulk. Beat the egg whites until stiff and fold them into the batter. Spoon a little into a hot waffle iron, close it immediately and turn it over to be sure the batter is evenly spread. Continue to heat the iron gently on each side until the waffles are done. When they are cold, serve them with whipped cream.

Brabo Fountain
Photo by Lee Snider/Photo Images

Recipes courtesy of The Embassy of Belgium

1
9
2
4

Boeuf à la Bourguignonne
Beef with Burgundy

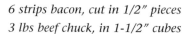

6 strips bacon, cut in 1/2" pieces
3 lbs beef chuck, in 1-1/2" cubes
1 large carrot, sliced
1 medium onion, sliced
3 tbsp all-purpose flour
2 cans condensed beef broth
2 cups red Burgundy wine
1 tbsp tomato paste
2 cloves garlic, minced
1/2 tsp thyme
1 bay leaf
1 quart (about 1 lb) mushrooms
1 lb small white onions

In dutch oven, cook bacon crisp; remove. Brown meat in the fat; remove. In drippings, brown carrot and onion. Spoon off fat; return bacon and beef to pan. Season with 1 tsp salt and 1/4 tsp pepper; stir in flour. Reserve 1/2 cup broth; add remainder to stew. Add wine, tomato paste and herbs. Cover; simmer 3 hours.

Quarter large mushrooms (leave small ones whole). Sauté in mixture of 3 tbsp butter and 2 tbsp salad oil for 5 minutes; lift out. Add small onions, brown; then add reserved broth; simmer covered until tender, about 10 minutes. Thicken stew with mixture of 1/4 cup flour in 1 cup water. Stir over very low heat until thick. Add mushrooms, onions; bring to bubbling. Serves 8 to 10.

Tourte de la Vallée
Valley Pie

Small sweet bun
milk
Clove of garlic
Finely chopped onion
Butter
Pork loin mince
1 egg
brandy
1 egg yolk

Soak a small sweet bun in some milk. Add a clove of garlic and finely chopped onion minced into butter and pork loin mince. Add one egg and brandy. Place the pastry in a dish and fill with the minced stuffing, making a chimney in the middle. Let it stand. Cover with the rest of the pastry, and brush with egg yolk. Bake in the oven at 350° for 35 minutes.

Tourte de la Vallée
Courtesy of Helio-Sud-Est/C. Kempf

Gestoofde Kabeljauw of Schelvis met Aardappelen
Baked Fillets of Haddock or Cod with Potatoes

2 onions, chopped
3 tbsp butter or margarine
6 fillets of haddock or cod
1 lb potatoes (3 medium), peeled
3 eggs
1/2 tsp salt
1 cup dairy sour cream
soft bread crumbs

Sauté onions in butter until golden brown. Flatten the fish into thin pieces. Boil potatoes for 10 minutes. Drain and slice. In a greased ovenproof dish layer fish with potatoes, sprinkling each layer with browned onions. End with a layer of potatoes. Beat eggs with salt for a few minutes. Add sour cream and pour over the fish. Sprinkle with bread crumbs. Bake in preheated moderate oven (350° F) for about 45 minutes. Makes 6 servings.

Gebakken Eieren met Uien en Kaas
Baked Eggs with Onions and Cheese

1 onion, grated
1/4 cup butter or margarine
1/4 cup grated cheddar cheese
6 eggs
1/2 cup medium cream

Sauté onion in the butter until golden brown. Sprinkle in shallow baking dish. Top onion with 2 tbsp cheese. Break eggs into baking dish, being careful to keep yolks whole. Cover with the cream and sprinkle with re-maining cheese. Bake in preheated moderate oven(350° F) for 15 minutes, or until eggs are of desired doneness. Makes 6 servings.

Kaastruffels
Cheese Truffles

1/2 cup butter
3 tbsp grated cheese
pepper, salt, celery salt, or paprika to taste
Slices of stale pumpernickel, crumbled into fine crumbs

Canal Sightseeing
Photo by Carl Purcell

Cream butter until light and fluffy. Mix in cheese and desired spices. Roll mixture into small balls about the size of a large olive. Roll balls in bread crumbs. Makes about 12. No cooking required.

*L*os Angeles, United States

Chicken and Yellow Rice

8 pieces of chicken

salt, pepper and garlic salt, to taste

1/2 cup lemon or lime juice

4 tbsp olive oil

2 medium onions, chopped

6 garlic cloves, minced

1/2 cup diced ham

1/2 can tomato paste (3 oz)

1 medium green pepper, diced

1 cup dry white wine

2 cups uncooked yellow rice

4 cups chicken broth

1 16-oz can tiny peas

1 small jar pimentos, chopped

Sprinkle chicken with salt, pepper and garlic salt. Pour lemon juice over chicken and marinate 4 hours, turning occasionally. Drain. Sauté chicken in olive oil in a 12" skillet, turning chicken so that it browns on both sides. Add onions, ground pepper to taste, garlic, ham, tomato paste and green pepper. Continue to sauté on medium heat until onions are transparent. Reduce to simmer. Add wine and simmer 2 to 3 minutes. Add rice and stir well so that rice is coated. Add chicken broth, stir and boil 1 minute. Cover and cook over low heat about 15 minutes. Add peas. Turn heat off and leave covered 15 minutes before serving. Garnish with pimentos. Serves 4.

Chicken and Yellow Rice
Photo by Joyce Oudkerk Pool

Fruit Soup

1 11 oz pkg (1-3/4 cups) mixed dried fruits

1/2 cup golden seedless raisins

1 stick cinnamon, 3-4"

4 cups water

1 medium orange, unpared, cut in 1/4" slices

1 No. 2 can (2-1/4 cups) unsweetened pineapple juice

1/2 cup currant jelly

1/4 cup sugar

2 tbsp quick-cooking tapioca

1/4 tsp salt

Combine mixed dried fruits, raisins, cinnamon, and water. Bring to boiling, then simmer uncovered until fruits are tender, about 30 minutes. Add remaining ingredients. Bring to a boil; cover, cook over low heat 15 minutes longer, stirring occasionally. Serve warm or chilled. Makes 8 to 10 servings.

Kartoffelsalat
Hot German Potato Salad

2 lbs cooked potato
4 strips minced bacon
1/4 cup chopped onion
1/4 cup chopped celery
1/4 cup vegetable stock
1/2 cup vinegar
1/2 tsp sugar
1/2 tsp dill weed
1/2 tsp salt
1/8 tsp paprika
1/4 tsp dry mustard

Take the potatoes and cook them with the skins on until tender. Peel and slice while hot. Cook bacon in a skillet; add onion and celery and sauté until golden color. Heat to boiling the stock and remaining ingredients. Combine all ingredients in skillet; gently stir with the potatoes. Serve at once with parsley. Leftovers can be served chilled.

Frankfurther Rippchen
Pot Roast of Smoked Loin of Pork

2 lbs smoked loin of pork
1 onion, chopped
1 tomato, chopped
1 celery stalk, chopped
1 cup water
salt and pepper

If necessary, cut loin into several pieces to fit a deep pot. Put meat into pot with remaining ingredients. Simmer, covered, for 1-1/2 hours. Add more water if necessary, but only just enough to prevent the meat from sticking. The cooking is really a steaming process. Serve with sauerkraut, mashed potatoes, and mustard. Makes 4 to 6 servings.

Opening Ceremonies
Courtesy of Landesbildstelle Berlin

11

London, England

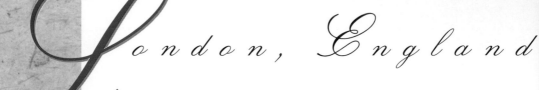

OLYMPIC GAMES

29 JULY 1948 14 AUGUST
LONDON

Steak and Kidney Pie

Puff pastry
2 lbs stewing steak
1 ox kidney (whole)
2 onions
flour
salt and pepper
2 tbsp butter

Melt butter in a saucepan. Add finely chopped onions, spread evenly over bottom of pan over low heat. Flour the chopped steak and kidneys and add to the saucepan. Leave, untouched, for approximately one hour on very low heat. Do not stir. When beef is cooked, add pepper and salt to taste and add water to cover the contents of the pan. Bring to the boil and then let cool. When cool, put into medium depth serving dish that is oven safe. Cover with puff pastry and decorate edges with fork. Bake at 450°F for 20-30 minutes or until pastry is cooked. Serves 4.

English Trifle

1 layer sponge cake or 1/2 tube chiffon cake
1/3 cup raspberry preserves or currant jelly
1/3 to 1/2 cup cooking sherry
1 1-lb can (2 cups) apricot halves, drained
1 3- or 3-1/4 oz package vanilla pudding
1 tsp vanilla
1/2 cup whipping cream, whipped
1/4 cup toasted slivered blanched almonds

Slice cake in 1/2" thick fingers; make into sandwiches, filling with preserves. Place half, spoke-fashion, in 1-1/2 quart serving dish. Sprinkle on half the sherry. Repeat with remaining cake (alternating with bottom spokes) and sherry. Quarter the apricot halves; place atop. Prepare pudding, following package directions, but using 3 cups milk. Remove from heat and stir in vanilla. While pudding is hot, pour over the dessert. Chill well. Before serving, center with whipped cream and nuts. Makes 8 servings.

The 1948 Olympic Games 200 m.
AllSport

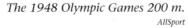

XVth OLYMPIC GAMES HELSINKI FINLAND 19·VII – 3·VIII·1952

Kaalikääryleet
Cabbage Rolls

a large cabbage
water
salt
Filling:
  1/2 cup raw rice
  water
  salt
  ground beef
  the core of the cabbage
  1 small onion, grated
  1/4 cup dried bread crumbs
  1/4 cup water
  1/4 cup cream
  salt, black pepper
  butter, margarine, or oil
  2 tbsp syrup
  water or bouillon

Cut out the core of the cabbage. Cook the cabbage in salted water until done. Remove the leaves and drain. Pare down the thick base of each leaf. Cook the rice in salted water. Let the bread crumbs swell in the water and cream mixture. Mix the ground beef, bread crumbs, onion, seasonings, and rice. Dice the core of the cabbage and add to the ground beef mixture. Season. Spread cabbage leaves on a board. Put 1-2 tablespoons of filling on each leaf. Wrap into little packages. Place the packages side by side in a greased baking dish. Top with a few dabs of butter and pour on syrup. Bake at 425° F until slightly brown. Turn and bake some more. Add water or bouillon. Lower the temperature to 350° F. Baste and bake for 45-60 minutes. Serve with lingonberry or cranberry jam or fresh puréed berries.

Recipes courtesy of the Embassy of Finland

Marjapuuro
Whipped Berry Porridge

4 cups water
1 cup lingonberry purée or 4 cups
  diluted, strong cowberry or cranberry juice
2/3 cup farina
2/3 cup sugar
1/4 tsp salt

Cook the berries and water to make a juice, then strain. Sweeten with sugar, add salt, and bring to a boil. Whip the farina into the boiling juice and cook for about 20 minutes. Let the porridge cool for a while in a cold water bath, then whip to make a light, pink dessert. Serve cold with milk.

Cabbage Rolls
Courtesy of the Embassy of Finland

Melbourne, Australia

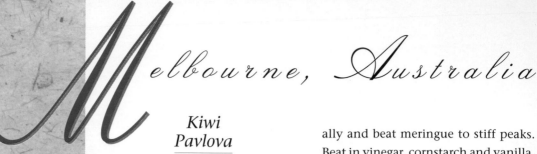

Kiwi Pavlova

Raspberry sorbet

Kiwi

Whipped cream

Meringue:

4 large egg whites

1/4 tsp salt

1/8 tsp cream of tartar

1 cup sugar

1 tbsp distilled or white vinegar

1 tbsp cornstarch

1 tsp vanilla

Preheat oven to 250° F and line baking sheet with parchment. In bowl, beat egg whites with salt and cream of tartar to soft peaks. Add sugar gradu- ally and beat meringue to stiff peaks. Beat in vinegar, cornstarch and vanilla. On prepared baking sheet spread meringue into 3-1/2" to 4" rows, making slightly higher around edges to make shells. Bake on low shelf of oven 1 hour or until crisp on outside. Peel parchment from meringues and cool on rack. Keep for one day in closed container. Serve meringues topped with sorbet, whipped cream, and kiwi. Serves 6.

"Down Under" Fish

1/2 lb fresh mushrooms

2 tbsp butter

1 tbsp oil

1/2 cup parmesan, cheddar or cheshire cheese

1-1/2 lbs fillet of sole (or any white fish)

1/4 tsp salt

1/4 tsp pepper

4 tbsp green pepper, chopped

6 tbsp white wine

2 tsp fresh lemon juice

1 tbsp fresh parsley, chopped

Melt butter in skillet over low heat. Add mushrooms and sauté over medium heat until tender. Rub oil over shallow 4-quart baking dish and sprinkle with grated cheese. Place fish on cheese. Sprinkle fish with salt and pepper. Add onions and top with mushrooms. Pour wine over fillets. Bake at 450° F for 20 minutes or until fish flakes. Sprinkle with lemon juice and parsley. Serves 4.

Melbourne
Photo courtesy of the Embassy of Australia

GAMES OF THE XVII OLYMPIAD
ROMA   25.VIII-11.IX

Zucchini Roma
Roman Zucchini

5 medium zucchini
1/4 cup flour
1 tsp salt
1 tsp oregano
1/4 tsp ground pepper
1/4 cup olive oil
1 cup sour cream
2 cups tomato sauce
1/2 cup parmesan cheese

Wash and scrub zucchini well. Cut into thin round pieces. Mix flour with half the salt, pepper and oregano in a bowl. Coat zucchini slices in mixture. Heat oil in a skillet and sauté zucchini until brown. Put zucchini in a greased baking dish and top with tomato sauce. Combine sour cream and the rest of the salt, oregano and pepper and spread over tomato sauce. Bake 30 minutes at 350° F. Serves 6.

Pollo Alla Cacciatora
Chicken Cacciatora

1/4 cup olive oil
1 2-1/2- to 3-pound ready-to-cook
    broiler-fryer chicken, cut up
2 medium onions, cut in 1/4" slices
2 cloves garlic, minced
1 1-pound can (2 cups) tomatoes
1 8-oz can seasoned tomato sauce
1 tsp salt
1/4 tsp pepper
1/2 tsp celery seed
1 tsp crushed oregano or basil
1 or 2 bay leaves
1/4 cup cooking sauterne

Heat olive oil in skillet; add chicken pieces; brown slowly, turning once. Remove chicken from skillet; cook onions and garlic in oil until tender, but not brown. Combine remaining ingredients except cooking wine. Return chicken to skillet, add sauce mixture. Cover and simmer 45 minutes. Stir in cooking wine. Cook uncovered, turning occasionally, 20 minutes or until fork-tender. Remove bay leaves; skim off excess fat. Serve chicken with sauce ladled over. Serves 4.

The Colosseum
Photo by Dennis Barnes

15

Tokyo, Japan

Sukiyaki

1 lb round steak
1/2 cup beef bouillon
3 tsp soy sauce
1/4 lb sliced mushroom
1/4 lb spinach
3 tbsp peanut oil
3/4 cup sliced celery
3/4 cup sliced onion
2 cups cooked rice

With a sharp knife, cut steaks across grain into diagonal strips about 3" long. Heat oil in a large skillet and brown with meat. Add bouillon mixture and push meat to one side. Add celery, mushrooms and onions. Stir and cook for about 4 minutes. Add the spinach and cook about 2 minutes more. Sprinkle with soy sauce. Serve on a bed of rice. Makes 4 servings.

Chawan-Mushi
Custard Soup

8 raw shrimp, peeled and deveined
8 spinach leaves, cut in 1-1/2" pieces
1/2 cup sliced fresh mushrooms
8 water chestnuts, sliced
2 slightly beaten eggs
2 cups canned chicken broth
1/2 tsp salt

Make small slit in each shrimp; pull tail through. Wilt spinach in hot water, drain. In each of eight 8-oz custard cups (or Chawan-Mushi cups), place shrimp, spinach, mushrooms, and water chestnuts. Combine eggs, chicken broth, and salt; pour into cups; cover with foil. Set cups on rack in dutch oven; pour hot water around cups 1 inch deep; cover to steam. Over medium heat, bring water slowly to simmering; reduce heat and cook 7 minutes or until knife inserted off center comes out clean. Top each custard with 1/4 teaspoon soy sauce and a twist of lemon peel.

TOKYO 1964

Opening Ceremonies
Allsport

Gazpacho

1 cup finely chopped peeled tomato
1/2 cup each finely chopped green
    pepper, celery, and cucumber
1/4 cup finely chopped onion
2 tsp snipped parsley
1 tsp snipped chives
1 small clove garlic, minced
2 to 3 tbsp tarragon wine vinegar
2 tbsp olive oil
1 tsp salt
1/4 tsp black pepper
1/2 tsp worcestershire sauce
2 cups tomato juice
Croutons:
    bread
    butter

Combine ingredients in stainless steel or glass bowl. Cover; chill at least 4 hours. Serve in chilled cups. Pass crisp croutons. Croutons: Cut slightly dry bread in 1/2" cubes. Melt a little butter in a skillet; add bread cubes; toss lightly. Heat and stir until croutons are golden brown. Makes 6 servings.

Huevos Picante

1 tbsp vegetable oil
1 small onion, chopped
1-2 cloves garlic, minced
1 jalapeño pepper, finely chopped, or
    1 4-oz can green chilies, drained &
    chopped
2 tomatoes, chopped
8 eggs
1 tbsp milk
1/3 cup broken corn chips
1/2 tsp salt
1/4 tsp black pepper

Using a 10" skillet, sauté onion, garlic, jalapeño pepper and tomatoes until onions are soft and transparent. Scramble eggs with milk and add to sautéed vegetables; add broken corn chips, salt and pepper; continue to cook and stir until eggs are barely moist. Serve immediately. Makes 6-8 servings.

Huevos Picante
Photo by Joyce Oudkerk Pool

Munich, Germany

Cherry Torte

2 8" sponge cake layers
2 1-oz square semi-sweet chocolate,
    shaved
Cherry Filling:
    1 1-lb can (2 cups) pitted dark
    sweet cherries
    1/3 cup kirsch
    1-1/2 tbsp cornstarch
Butter creme:
    1/2 lb soft butter
    4-1/2 cups confectioners sugar,
    sifted
    3 egg yolks

Filling: Drain cherries, reserving 3/4 cup syrup. Pour kirsch over halved cherries. Let stand two hours. Place cornstarch in pan, blend in remaining syrup, add cherry mixture. Bring to boil, stirring constantly, for one minute. Cool. Chill.

Butter Creme: Beat butter and confectioner's sugar until smooth; beat in egg yolks until light and fluffy.

Cake: Place one sponge cake layer on plate. With one cup butter creme, make a 3/4" border around cake 1" high. Fill center with cherries. Place second layer on top. Cover top and sides with remaining butter creme. Sprinkle top and sides with shaved chocolate. Garnish with maraschino cherries. Chill. Serves 8.

Schnitzel

8 small veal cutlets (boneless)
thin slice ham
thin slice cheese

Pound the veal cutlets until very thin. Place a slice each of ham and cheese on four of the cutlets. Top with another cutlet. Roll in flour, then in beaten egg, and then in dry bread crumbs. Sauté quickly in hot fat to a golden brown on each side. Serves 4.

The Olympic Village
Courtesy of the Munich Tourist Office

Montréal, Canada

Tourtiere
Meat Pie

1 lb of meat
1 lb of ground lean pork or half pork-
  veal or half pork-beef
1/2 cup of water (approximately)
1 chopped onion
1 chopped garlic clove (to taste)
salt, pepper, cloves (to taste)
1 cooked mashed potato (no butter
  or milk)
Dough for top and bottom

Mix all ingredients except dough and cook over medium heat for about 20 minutes (add water if necessary). Add the mashed potato and mix well (taste and season if necessary).

Preheat oven 350° F. Bake as a pie (dough on top and bottom) until golden brown. Delicious with home-made ketchup or Heinz 57.

Camembert Frit
French-Fried Camembert

Camembert*
Crust
Egg, beaten
Fine dry bread crumbs

Cut six 1-1/3 ounce triangles of Camembert* in half lengthwise, then crosswise (24 pieces). Shape crust around soft center so it covers as much of center as possible. Dip in beaten egg, then in fine dry bread crumbs, then again in egg and crumbs. (A thick coat of crumbs prevents the cheese from leaking through.)

Fry in deep hot fat (375° F) until crumbs are crisp and golden brown. Drain and serve hot on small plates. Offer picks or forks.

*Or use Port du Salut. Cut in bite-size pieces or cut with melon-ball cutter; mold into small balls. Coat and fry.

The Olympic Stadium
Courtesy of the Greater Montréal Convention and Tourism Bureau

Moscow, Soviet Union

OLYMPIAD 80
MOSCOU MOSCOW МОСКВА

Chicken Kiev

4 medium chicken breasts

1 tbsp each chopped green onion and parsley

1/4 lb butter

Flour

2 eggs, beaten

1 cup fine dry bread crumbs

Cut chicken breasts lengthwise in half. Remove the skin and cut away the bone. Be careful not to tear the meat—each half should be all in one piece. Place each piece of chicken, boned side up, between two pieces of clear plastic wrap. Working out from center, pound with wooden mallet to form cutlets not quite 1/4" thick. Peel off wrap. Sprinkle with salt. Sprinkle green onion and parsley over cutlets. Cut butter into 8 sticks. Place a stick at end of each cutlet. Roll meat like a jellyroll, tucking in sides. Press end to seal well. Dust each roll with flour and dip in beaten egg, then roll in bread crumbs. Chill thoroughly, at least 1 hour. Fry chicken rolls in deep, hot fat (340° F) about 5 minutes or until golden brown. Serve with mushroom sauce and pass lemon wedges if desired. Makes 4-6 servings.

Borscht

5 beets

1-1/2 quarts water

1 chopped onion

1 cup tomato purée

1 tbsp lemon juice

1 tsp sugar

1/2 tsp dill weed

salt

pepper

sour cream or yogurt (optional)

Peel and grate beets. Combine with onion and water in a heavy kettle. Bring to a boil; cover and simmer about 45 minutes. Add tomato, lemon juice, dill, salt and pepper. Cook 45 minutes more. Heat but do not boil. Serve hot or cold topped with sour cream or low fat plain yogurt. Serves 4-6.

St. Peter's Basilica
Photo by Bob Giandomenico/VisionQuest

Black Bean Soup

3 cups black beans

6 cups water

7 cups vegetable broth

1 large (28 oz) can cut-up tomatoes,
    including liquid

2 cups chopped celery

1 large chopped carrot

1 large chopped onion

4 large minced garlic cloves

2 bay leaves

1 tsp oregano

1 tsp basil

1/2 tsp marjoram

1-1/2 tbsp lemon juice

5-1/2 tbsp sherry

5 tbsp vinegar

3 tbsp worcestershire sauce

2 tbsp parsley

sour cream (optional)

chives

Rinse beans, discarding discolored ones. Soak overnight in water in saucepan. Strain and refill with vegetable broth. Add all remaining ingredients to marjoram. Simmer for 2 to 2-1/2 hours until beans are soft. Add the rest of the ingredients except sour cream and chives. Remove bay leaves, blend soup in blender. Return to soup pot. Reheat and serve. May garnish each serving with 1 tablespoon cream and a sprinkling of chives.

Broiled Tofu

1" chunk of ginger root

1 tbsp tamari

1 tbsp sesame oil

water

1 tbsp lemon juice

1/2 lb tofu, sliced 1/4" thick

chopped scallions or parsley

Rinse and grate ginger and squeeze out juice. Mix juice with tamari and oil. Dilute two parts sauce with one part water. Add lemon juice. Pour over tofu. Broil 5 to 7 minutes and garnish with scallions or parsley. Serves 2.

Los Angelos Memorial Coliseum
Photo by B. Mitock

Seoul, Korea

Pulgogi
Korean Bar-B-Que

3 lbs or more sirloin, sliced very thin
1 cup soy sauce
1-2 tbsp sugar
1 clove garlic, minced
1/4 cup sesame oil
1 tsp sesame seeds
2 chopped green onions
black pepper to taste

Mix all ingredients and marinate with sirloin for at least 1/2 hour. Then grill on outdoor grill. Accompany with assorted vegetables. Put whatever vegetables you like on a lettuce leaf, add Bar-B-Que beef on top. Wrap lettuce around all the ingredients. Enjoy! Makes 4 servings.

Pulgogi
Courtesy of the Consulate of the Republic of Korea

Kim Chi

1 Napa (China Kohl)
3 tbsp salt (for pickling)
1 tbsp salt
1 tbsp sugar
1 tbsp garlic (ground)
1 tsp ginger (ground)
1 tbsp anchovy or shrimp sauce
3 tbsp powdered red pepper
3 tbsp water
3 green onions

Cup the napa in 1-1/2" pieces. Wash well. Pickle napa with pickling salt for two hours. Rinse well, drain water. Soak powdered red pepper in water for 30 minutes. Cut green onions into small pieces. Put all ingredients into napa, mix well. Store at room temperature for two days, then keep refrigerated

City of Seoul
Photo by J. Joseph

Paella

1 2-lb cut chicken
1/4 cup peanut oil
1/4 cup water
1/2 cup chopped onion
1 clove crushed garlic
2 cups uncooked rice
1/4 tsp saffron
4 cups chicken broth
1 lb cooked shrimp
1/2 lb Italian sausage
15 clams
1 cup thawed frozen peas

Cut chicken and brown all over with oil in a large skillet Add water, cover and simmer for 30 minutes. Remove chicken and set aside.

In the same skillet, add onion and garlic; sauté until clear. Add rice and saffron; cook over low heat until rice is light brown. Add chicken broth, bring to a boil, cover, reduce heat and simmer about 17 minutes. Toss in peas. Arrange rice, chicken, shrimp, sausage and clams in layers and place in a large oiled casserole dish. Bake at 350° F for 15-20 minutes. If using clams, bake until they open.

Merluza Asada al Horno
Baked fish

1 to 1-1/2 lbs fish fillets
1/2 cup olive oil
2 onions, chopped fine
2 garlic cloves, minced
salt and pepper to taste
2 medium tomatoes, chopped
1/4 to 1/2 cup dry white wine
2 tbsp chopped parsley
juice of 1 lemon
3 cups cooked rice

Pour 2/3 oil into a baking dish. Spread an even layer of half the onion and garlic in dish and lay the fish on top. Sprinkle with salt and pepper and the remaining onion, garlic, and oil. Add chopped tomatoes and wine. Bake in preheated hot oven (400° F), allowing 12 minutes per pound. Before serving, sprinkle fish with parsley and lemon juice. Serve over hot cooked rice. Makes 6 servings.

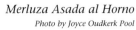

Merluza Asada al Horno
Photo by Joyce Oudkerk Pool

Atlanta, United States

Frozen Fruit Salad

1 quart fruit, diced small, using
   white cherries, sliced pineapple,
   canned pears
1 cup chopped pecan meats
1 cup mayonnaise
2 cups juice from the fruit
1 tsp salt

Mix together, then freeze. Serve on lettuce with dressing made of equal parts of mayonnaise and whipped cream. Lemon juice may be added to salad if too sweet.

Asparagus, Plain

Scrape, clean and boil asparagus in salt water until tender, about 30 minutes, drain and serve with white sauce or melted butter to which has been added salt, pepper and lemon juice. Have dish hot before putting asparagus into it.

Twentieth Century Pound Cake

4 cups flour, sifted
2 cups sugar
1 cup butter (1/2 lb)
1 cup water or milk
6 eggs
1/2 tsp vanilla extract
1/2 tsp lemon extract
2 tsp baking powder

Cream butter and sugar well. Add eggs, one at a time, beating constantly between eggs. Add flour and water alternately until all is in and smooth. Add flavorings. Sift baking powder and mix into batter. Put in a greased and papered pan—one with a steeple is best. Bake in a moderate oven 1-1/2 hours. This can be made into layers and baked as layers in a quick oven. By using 1/2 teaspoon of soda and 1 cup of buttermilk, some like it better leaving out all of the baking powder. Use the buttermilk in place of the water or sweet milk. Dissolve soda in one tablespoon of cold water, add last and mix well; put into pans.

Chicken Salad

2 cups cold cooked chicken, cut up
1 cup celery, cut up
1 tbsp lemon juice
1/2 cup mayonnaise
2 hard cooked eggs, cut up
salt and pepper to taste
Lettuce leaves

Mix chicken, celery, lemon juice, salt and pepper together. Add in mayonnaise. Carefully fold in eggs. Chill. Arrange a scoop full on each lettuce cup.

A Georgian Supper
Photo courtesy of Terrell Publishing